EUROPEAN INFLUENCE

PHOTOGRAPHS

Elliott McDowell

DAVID R. GODINE, PUBLISHER · BOSTON

First published in 1981 by
David R. Godine, Publisher
306 Dartmouth Street
Boston, Massachusetts 02116

LC 81-6604

Designed by Lance Hidy, Lancaster, N.H.
Printed by Gardner-Fulmer Lithograph,
Buena Park, California

Printed in the United States of America

Dedicated to my audience.

MISS KERR

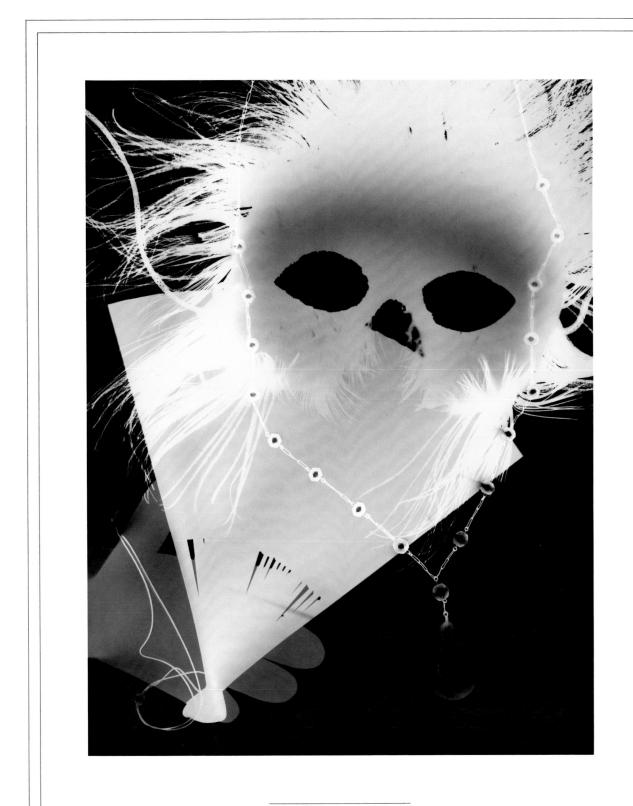

PHOTOGRAM NO. 6

THE DOLL HOUSE

TIWANAKU

ALFRED, THE BENTON CLUB

SPORTS FIGURES, COBB STADIUM

FLEETWOOD, NEW MEXICO

SKATELAND

BANANA SPLIT

ROOM SERVICE

RON

WHITE FACE

PHOTOGRAM NO. 3

SCENIC AIRLINE

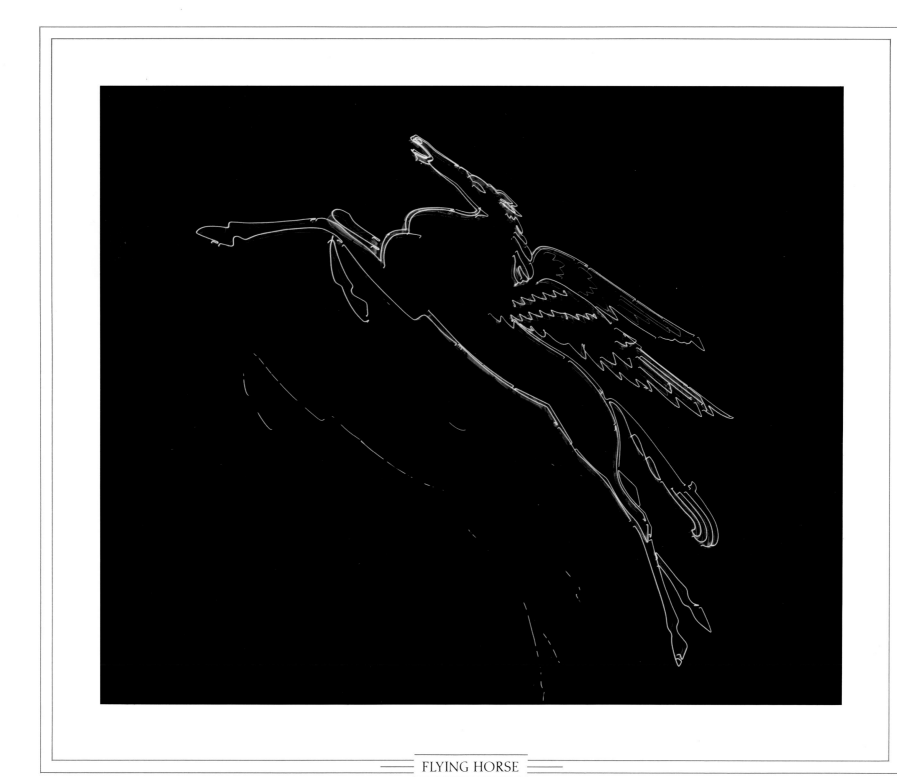

FLYING HORSE

A TINY SHIP ON A LARGE SEA

PHOTOGRAM NO. 7, GARDEN OF THE GODS

CULVERTS, NEW MEXICO

DESSERTS

PHOTOGRAM NO. 2

REHEARSAL DINNER

BOOTS AND WURLITZER

MELISSA IN THE LOBBY OF THE FAIRMONT

LOVE BIRDS

HAMILTON BEACH, NEW MEXICO

JOSIE'S

TEEPEES AND PALM TREES

PALM BEACH

PIANO AND CHAIR

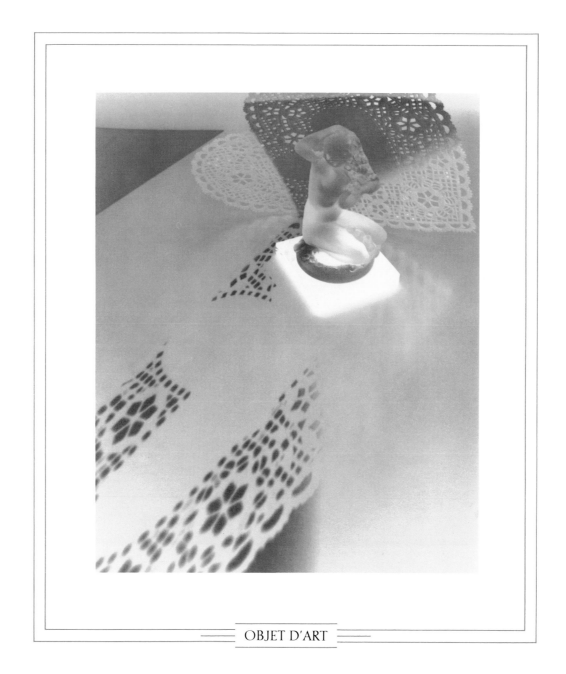

OBJET D'ART

AFTER A WEDDING

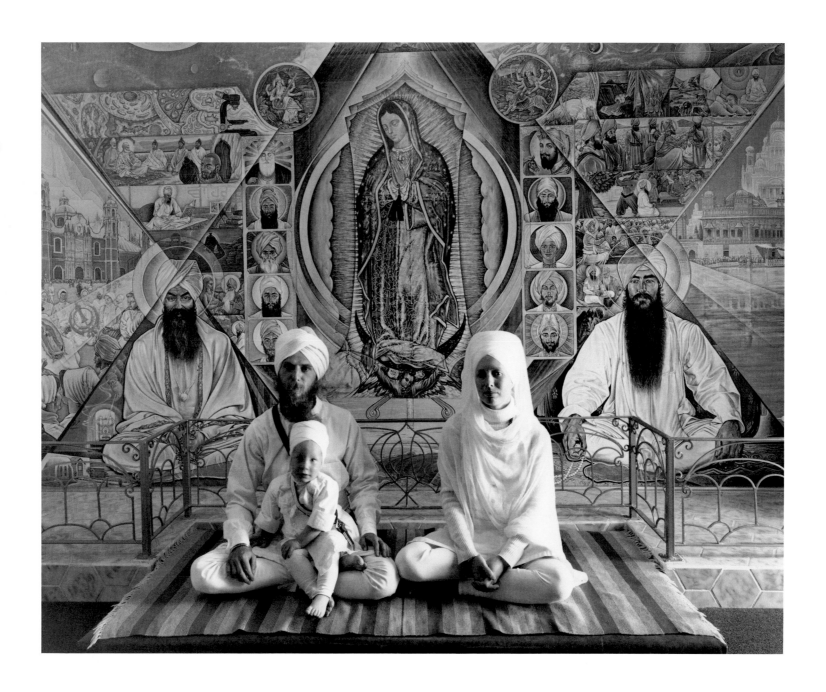

FAMILY PORTRAIT

THE SHADOW

MT. MORA

MOONRISE OVER ROLLS ROYCE

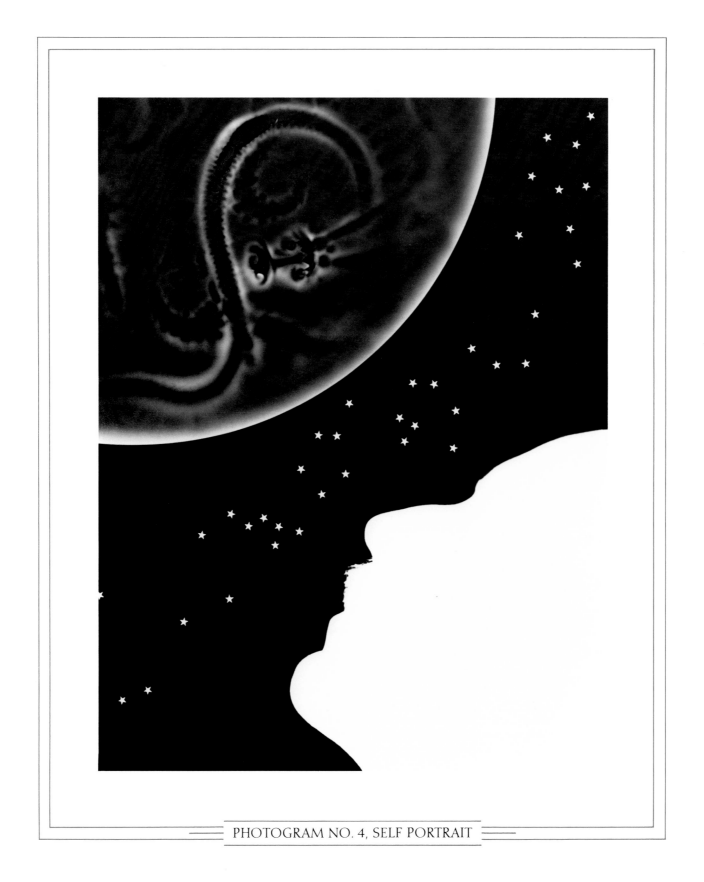

PHOTOGRAM NO. 4, SELF PORTRAIT

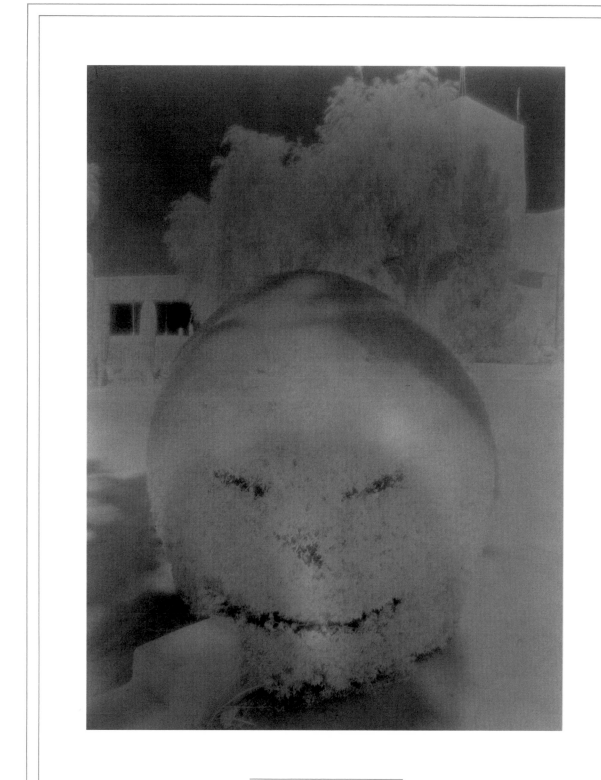

THE SMILING SHRUB

MINOX SAGUARO

Afterword

The purpose of this book is to entertain and communicate with the audience. My intention is to give the reader a pleasurable experience.

I am grateful to those professionals who have contributed creativity, knowledge, and expertise to enable this project to be completed. My sincere thanks to my family and friends who have supported my efforts over the years. Special love and appreciation to my wife Susan, who truly takes care of me and keeps me on the right path.

E.M.

People asking questions lost in confusion
Well I tell them there's no problem, only solutions
Well they shake their heads and look at me as if I've lost my mind
I tell them there's no hurry...
*I'm just sitting here doing time**

John Lennon

MY SHOE AND CARD